Five Seven Five

Erik Black

Published by Erik Black, 2024.

FIVE SEVEN FIVE

First edition. March 23, 2024.

Copyright © 2024 Erik Black.

ISBN: 979-8224483310

Written by Erik Black.

This book is dedicated to my mom who received my first haiku and encouraged my poetry ever since, and to my dad who trades haiku with me and has cheered me on in my writing.

Kanji on the cover by James Cermak

FIVE SEVEN FIVE

written for Mother's Day when I was in third grade

Haiku are an elegant form of poetry, and their simplicity and conciseness allow the writer to express a lot with very few words. In English the most common type of haiku has 3 lines with 17 syllables total: 5 on the first and third lines and 7 on the middle line. Traditional Japanese haiku had nature as their theme, while modern haiku explore a broader range of themes and sometimes vary the syllable count. A similar form to the haik is a senryū which usually has the same syllable count but is focused on themes of human nature rather than the natural world. Many of my poems here would fall under that category.

Since there is a difference between syllables in Japanese and English, some writers will reduce the count in their haiku to more closely approximate the sound or feel of a traditional haiku. A 2-3-2 or 3-5-3 syllable count forces the English poet to be even more precise with their words:

one step
too many
fell down

Christmas scent
sugar and spice and
all things nice

The haiku, like all poetic forms, is merely a means to convey an image or idea or sentiment. Though I normally compose poetry in free verse, I enjoy the challenge of trying to say more with less. I find that the boundaries of the haiku form bring a freedom of expression.

Most of these poems are untitled, a rare thing for me, and most do not rhyme (not so rare for me). Of note is a series of haiku I composed in December 2022 as a challenge to write one every day. I chose to include all of them to show that some days are better than others in poetry as in life. The first two haiku are from my previous book, Ink of Serendipity.

tsundoku
piles and piles for miles
a catastrophe of my
literary mind

wabi-sabi
tender ugly scar
reminder of the faith leap
regrets left behind

spring snow, winter rain
how the snow lingers
little patch of gray white ice
in my rain drenched lawn

the steam swirling up,
a murmuring of starlings
from my morning tea

city hawk
shadow on the wing
swift flyer on urban winds
seen out my window

tree
pushing upwards from
the unmoving earth, reaching
for the circling sun

inland passage
sparkled jewels float
upon the shivering sea
left by clouded sun

ghosts walk among us
pale shadows of former life
i am one of them

transience of white
snow hanging on dark branches
sun waking the day

HAIKU DECEMBER!!
12/1
December, winter
now upon us, enter the
time of dark and light

12/2
disturbing brightness
of the winter morning sun
piercing my tired eyes

12/3
Homburg on my head,
glimmering beauty near my
ever grateful soul

12/4 (after seeing Wakanda Forever)
a panther prowling
beyond this mortal coil's reach
his presence felt still

12/5
office window view
buildings taller than me, still
nothing like the trees

12/6
traitorous fluffball
jumping to another lap
mine was free for you

12/7
the sum of my head
all ten thousand crazy thoughts
these i give to you

12/8
five minute parking
at the busy DMV
what were they thinking?

12/9
Chartreuse bottle gone
last of the night's cocktail drinks
shared among old friends

12/10
Christmas tree twinkling
light dancing upon your head
and your light to me

12/11
overnight the lawn
has aged from brown to near white
winter upon it

12/12
disorganized life
inside and outside my head
no hope for restart

12/13
Saint Lucia Day
candles dripping from her crown
before childhood dawn

12/14
swirling and droning
the constant refrain saying
he's not good enough

12/15
screaming out his song
blue feathers against gray sky
bird cacophony

12/16
love is a plateau -
not meaning to cease growing
but a height attained

12/17
memory fading
did i write these lines before?
memory failing

12/18 (for Frank my sourdough starter)
ten million Frank friends
slow to rise in the morning
but reach heights in heat

12/19
too few snow flurries
dancing in the winter sky
gray hope tomorrow

12/20
coming or going
always one or the other
our reality

12/21
pending winter storm
hope for blanket of bright white
anticipation

12/22
bird feeding frenzy
staving off the frigid chill
fly another day

12/23
bright color and song
orange breast against snowy deck
my favorite finch

12/24
i am left alone
on this eve of Christmas day
tomorrow brings joy

12/25
i've no Christmas peace
kitchen a bustle of work
dinner gift to all

12/26
patterns on a lake
ice floe upon dark waters
winter harmony

12/27
crescent moon a bowl
spilling starlight and gray clouds
light and shadow swirl

12/28
the songs in his head
overlapping lives and notes
noisy symphonies

12/29
warm in December
snow melted in the soft breeze
respite from winter

12/30
should be slumbering
dreaming of the days ahead
again i can't sleep

12/31
a day for singing
and ringing and bringing in
a new year of hope

43

1/1
a new year today
same birds on my deck feeding
just another day

casting cares upon
the Rhine, he looks to find they
have followed downstream

45

wind nipped finger tips
a dearth of trout in the hand
bliss of fly fishing

i have cast white clouds
upon bay waters, rippled
reflections of sky

47

feet wet with the sea
i have walked upon the waves
following the One

48

shortbread
three ingredients
butter, flour and brown sugar
sum greater than all

blackout Christmas Eve
no sound but the falling rain
my peaceful morning

Christmas Eve with you
twinkling lights, warmth and good food
blessings of us two

anticipation
snowfall on the horizon
childhood saudade

2 a.m. snow light
falling into my bedroom
joy awakening

streetlight in the fog
a scene from cinema noir
shadows in the dark

dimming the future
his body steady failing
still She beside him

i hate this body
see the failures day by day
fear the looming weak

memory walking
deep sleep evading my mind
past and future meet

57

behold the mundane
dreary monotonous days
springboard for dreaming

memento mori
carried in this old body
every day a gift

dun fly above them
young one takes and is netted
educating trout

joy in creation
each poem, painting or song
the artist's passion

time change
i may sleep again
it happens from time to time
too early to rise

For Kenneth (Mitchell)
flying without wings
you among the stars for us
lift our hearts and eyes

63

happy is that man
seeing riches all around
is content with his

drinking his sorrows
a fine wine aged past it's prime
sipping bitterness

red bird darkened to
blood shadow, early morning
against new snow fall

red bird darkened to
blood shadow, early morning
against new snow fall

hummingbird sipping
from white raspberry flowers
tiny sustenance

67

unexplained sadness
a darkness on the edges
as of torn paper

Dasha
kitty sits pretty
regurgitates her breakfast
a present for you

Pushkin
kitty lies dozing
fluffy mane of royalty
kings need their sleep too

fountain pen in hand
paper ready to receive
inky words and dreams

creature of habit
seldom strays from what she knows
okay if I'm hers

trout are my first love
not to eat, though that is sweet
but to catch, divine

Spring peepers chorus
their pond is four houses down
backyard symphony

the shirts i have worn
banners of my allegiance
now on the top shelf

1
wandering forward
to see all that i can see
paths of potential
2
wandering backward
to see all that i have missed
paths of memory

Also by Erik Black

Glacial Dreams
A Paradox of Shadows
The Trees Were Spinning
Ink of Serendipity
Five Seven Five